PUBLISHING
& associates

What to Do
when life
Doesn't Turn Out Like You Planned

DAVID HARRIS

PUBLISHING
& associates

What to Do When Life Doesn't Turn Out Like You Planned
ISBN PRINT: 978-1-944566-39-5
ISBN EBOOK: 978-1-944566-40-1
Copyright © 2023 Bush Publishing & Associates

Bush Publishing & Associates, LLC books may be ordered at everywhere and at Amazon.com
For further information, please contact:
Bush Publishing & Associates
Tulsa, Oklahoma
www.bushpublishing.com

Printed in the United States of America.

DEDICATION

Helping people understand and respond to this message is my life's work. It came as a sheer gift to me, a real surprise, God handling all the details. When it came to presenting the Message to people who had no background in God's way, I was the least qualified of any of the available Christians. God saw to it that I was equipped, but you can be sure that it had nothing to do with my natural abilities.

"And so here I am, preaching and writing about things that are way over my head, the inexhaustible riches and generosity of Christ. My task is to bring out in the open and make plain what God, who created all this in the first place, has been doing in secret and behind the scenes all along." Ephesians 3:7-9 (MSG)

A dear saint of God, and great prayer warrior, Ms. Anne Brown, gave me the above passage of scripture from the Message Bible in September 2017. She titled it simply "The Word of God to Pastor David". This book and subsequent works that I hope to publish, are the fulfillment of this prophetic word. Ms. Anne has since gone on to be with the Lord. This book is dedicated to her loving memory as her prayers and words of encouragement continue to bear fruit.

CONTENT

1

MY LIFE DIDN'T TURN
OUT LIKE I PLANNED

*This really should be the introduction. If you're like me,
sometimes we skip the introduction, preface and foreword.
But I didn't want to risk anyone missing out on this.*

I planned on writing a book. Just not THIS book. About THIS subject. I wanted to write a book titled *How to Have a Successful Marriage* or *How to Be a Great Dad* or maybe *Five Keys to Being a Success in Ministry*. Those would be fun books to write. Writing books like that makes us all feel good. But I didn't ever plan to write THIS book, *What to Do When Life Doesn't Turn Out Like You Planned*. No one wants to write this book. No one wants to have to admit their failures, sins and short-comings. Yet, this *is* my story, and I have lived and experienced this message. If your life hasn't turned out like you planned, I pray that by the grace and goodness of God, this will bring hope to you.

What Happened???

I was blessed with a marvelous family. I had a beautiful, wonderful, godly wife, who gave me five amazing children. I was privileged to pastor a fantastic church. Looking back, I didn't realize how blessed I was. Here's the big question… With all that I just mentioned, what happened?! Life seemed so wonderful and perfect, so why did I wake up one day only to realize that life had not turned out like I planned?

A combination of issues contributed to how I ended up in such a bad place in my life. They ranged from the pressures and busy-ness of the ministry, to neglecting to properly take care of my wife's heart and nurture our relationship. Looking back, I realized I had allowed hurt and rejection in ministry to turn to bitterness in my heart, causing me to wind up in a bad place spiritually and emotionally. I made some very bad decisions in the middle of that state of mind. Selfish decisions. From that place, my choices led to me betraying my wife, and as a result that brought devastating emotional pain and confusion to my children. In turn, that brought disappointment and sadness to people who called me their pastor.

I woke up one day, and thought that my life was over. But God…

As He is so faithful to do when we are right in the middle of a place of despair, realizing we have blown it, God came to me in the form of His word.. We often speak of "finding a scripture" that speaks to our life or situation, but I have to say in my case these scriptures FOUND ME. There are too many to list here, but each one spoke directly to my heart, to my situation. They are His exceedingly great and precious promises. Sometimes I stumbled across them during my daily Bible reading. Others came as the Holy Spirit whispered to my heart "Remember what My Word says in"...and the Holy Spirit would lead me to one scripture after another. Each one gave me HOPE that my life was not over. Even though things had not turned out like I planned, God was still at work to redeem, restore and rebuild my life if I would only cooperate with Him.

Maybe this has spoken to you already. Perhaps you too wandered off the path like I did. Now you are away from the good plan and blessings God intended for your life because of your sin, disobedience and hardness of heart. Or maybe the actions of other people have damaged you and caused loss in your life. That can happen too. Or perhaps destruction came into your life as a direct attack and onslaught of Satan. I want to share with you some key parts of my personal story, along with several examples given to us in scripture of people whose life didn't turn out like they planned. As we look at these, we are going to discover divine principles of recovery and restoration, to get our lives back on track. These are the principles that God gave me, to apply in my life. And they have worked! Your life may have ended up where you didn't plan. But your story is NOT OVER! There is a God who loves you, who is at work even now, and your story can end "and they lived happily ever after"!

2

THE STORY OF NAOMI
When Life Has Left You Bitter

"Now it came to pass, in the days when the judges ruled, that there was a famine in the land. And a certain man of Bethlehem, Judah, went to dwell in the country of Moab, he and his wife and his two sons. 2 The name of the man was Elimelech, the name of his wife was Naomi, and the names of his two sons were Mahlon and Chilion — Ephrathites of Bethlehem, Judah. And they went to the country of Moab and remained there. 3 Then Elimelech, Naomi's husband, died; and she was left, and her two sons. 4 Now they took wives of the women of Moab: the name of the one was Orpah, and the name of the other was Ruth. And they dwelt there about ten years. 5 Then both Mahlon and Chilion also died; so the woman survived her two sons and her husband." –Ruth 1:1-5 NKJV

We are looking at scripture in the book of Ruth. Ruth herself has an amazing story, but this is also the story of Naomi. At one time, Naomi and her family made the decision to leave their homeland (the land of Israel) because of a famine. They went to the land of Moab, and Naomi's husband died. Then both of her sons died. Life was surely not turning out like Naomi planned!

You may have come to a place in your life, maybe you are there now, where you have said, "Wow, this is not what I had planned, this is not how I thought my life would turn out."

Perhaps you have faced the loss of your job, maybe a career field you have worked in all your life, and now you're age 50 or 60 and you wonder what you're going to do because life didn't turn out like you planned.

Or maybe you have a wayward child, struggling with addiction, maybe they are incarcerated, and you think back to when they were a child growing up, with such hope and promise, and you say to yourself, "I surely never wanted things to turn out this way."

Perhaps you have gone through a divorce, as I have. No one plans for that. No one says "Well, let's be married for a few years, then get a divorce." No one wants life to turn out like that.

We ALL face situations in our lives where life just doesn't turn out like we planned.

Here is the key question: Now what? What will we do? How will we respond?

Let's look at Naomi's story and find out what she did, and discover Biblical principles that apply to our situations today.

After the deaths of her husband and her sons, Naomi decided to return to the land of Israel. She told her daughter-in-laws to stay in the land of Moab, and find husbands there. But Ruth would not be persuaded. She decided to follow Naomi to the land of Israel.

They went back to Naomi's hometown, and all of her old friends recognized her and rushed to greet her and welcome her home. They joyfully spread the word "Naomi is back, Naomi is home!" But Naomi quells their joy and excitement with these words:

Ruth 1:20-21 NKJV

20 "But she said to them, "Do not call me Naomi; call me Mara, for the Almighty has dealt very bitterly with me. 21 I went out full, and the Lord has brought me home again empty. Why do you call me Naomi, since the Lord has testified against me, and the Almighty has afflicted me?"

Naomi means PLEASANT. Mara means BITTER. Naomi declared "My life is no longer pleasant, my life is bitter."

We all want life to turn out *PLEASANT* for us, don't we? Yet sometimes it doesn't. It can make us bitter. It can cause us to abandon faith and lose hope. Naomi blamed God, saying "The

Almighty has dealt very bitterly with me." and "The Almighty has afflicted me." My friend, don't let a root of bitterness grow in your life. Don't get cynical. Don't let go of your faith. Stay with God.

Principle #1. Stay on God's Side, He is NOT your problem.

The Bible says that Satan is the "accuser of the brethren", accusing us before God. But he also attempts to accuse God to the brethren, telling us that God is our problem, and that God caused our tragedy. Don't buy his lie! Reject his accusation! God is good! God is FOR YOU. God is your answer! Stay on His side!

Think about it. God was not to blame for the famine, or for them becoming refugees or for her husband and sons dying. Even though she couldn't see it, God was already WORKING His plan to cause things to turn out GOOD for Naomi in the end.

No, it wasn't going to bring her husband or her sons back. There may be losses in life that we suffer and are unable to return back to living the way things were before. But that doesn't mean that our future can't be bright, and that our story won't have a happy and blessed ending!

Principle #2. Assess Your Situation – Why Are You Where You Are?

No One Plans to Fail, But Many Fail to Plan

Maybe the reason things haven't turned out like you planned is that you didn't really have a PLAN. Maybe you had a dream, or an ideal image of how things ought to be. But we do need to PLAN, and we need to have FOCUS and that will help us to live with PURPOSE. Today people use the phrase "live intentionally".

Let's step away from Naomi for a moment, and look at Noah, to understand the importance of a plan.

Hebrews 11:7 NKJV

7 "By faith Noah, being divinely warned of things not yet seen, moved with godly fear, prepared an ark for the saving of his household"...

Think about it. Noah had a PLAN when he built the Ark. He diligently followed that plan, day after day for 120 years until the Ark was completed! The end result was that he and his family were SAVED while the rest of humanity perished!

Did Noah just come up with the plan on his own? We see from scripture that God revealed to him the plan!

Genesis 6:14-16 NKJV

14 "Make yourself an ark of gopherwood; make rooms in the ark, and cover it inside and outside with pitch. 15 And this is how you shall make it: The length of the ark shall be three hundred cubits, its width fifty cubits, and its height thirty cubits. 16 You shall make a window for the ark, and you shall finish it to a cubit from above; and set the door of the ark in its side. You shall make it with lower, second, and third decks."

God has a plan for YOU to follow for the saving of YOUR household, and for your life to be blessed, fruitful and full of purpose. You'll discover His plan as you read His word, and as you pray and open your heart to Him.

If you don't have a plan for your life and your family, and I'm speaking of a plan that has come from God and from His Word, then you will be susceptible to getting caught up in the flow of life. It's so easy to get pulled into the busy-ness of life and wake up one day thinking, "How did I end up here?"

Make sure you are following God's plan!

Things Don't Turn Out Like We Planned Because of Our Wrong Decisions

Proverbs 19:3 NLT

3 "People ruin their lives by their own foolishness and then are angry at the Lord."

Don't blame God! He is not your problem.

If things haven't turned out like you planned, then TAKE OWNERSHIP!

Principle #3. Take Ownership of Your Life

It didn't take long after God created Adam and Eve, and placed them in the garden of Eden where everything was total perfection, for things to go wrong. Life took a horrible turn and did NOT go as Adam and Eve had planned, and especially as God had planned for them.

10

Genesis 3:9-12 NKJV

9 "Then the Lord God called to Adam and said to him, "Where are you?"

10 So he said, "I heard Your voice in the garden, and I was afraid because I was naked; and I hid myself."

11 And He said, "Who told you that you were naked? Have you eaten from the tree of which I commanded you that you should not eat?"

12 Then the man said, "The woman whom You gave to be with me, she gave me of the tree, and I ate."

Adam blamed Eve AND God! Think about it! In verse 12, after God gave him an opportunity to take responsibility for his actions, he blamed Eve, and then said "By the way God, she was YOUR idea, not mine!"

Genesis 3:13 NKJV

13 "And the Lord God said to the woman, "What is this you have done?"

The woman said, "The serpent deceived me, and I ate."

When God turned to Eve, and gave her an opportunity to be accountable, she tried to blame it all on the devil.

If we are going to recover and get back on track when life hasn't turned out as we planned, we must FIRST look in the mirror, and take ownership of our lives.

Know that God loves you! Know that He wants to forgive and restore you and fix the mess that you have made. But you must be honest and acknowledge your part and be willing to make corrections. Corrections in your thinking, your habits and your decisions.

A Supernatural Experience:

I remember in my own situation, a particularly powerful experience I had with the Lord. I had already repented and had grieved over my sin, shedding many tears, but then I had an unforgettable experience. An awareness of the enormity and the magnitude of my sin and all the people I had hurt, came crashing down upon me like an overwhelming crushing weight. I visualized it as a ceiling collapsing all over me and around me. I despaired as I tried to hold it up, but in hopelessness I realized it was impossible. I could not fix what I had done. I could not undo it. I cried out to God in desperation, feeling the weight of guilt "Oh God I can't lift this, I can't fix this." As I said that, He spoke to my heart "Yes, I know…but I CAN!" And I immediately felt the weight lift off of me!

God needs us to acknowledge our sin and our part in what went wrong. When we truly repent, He does NOT want us to continue to live under the load of guilt and shame. He lifts it off of us through the cleansing blood of Jesus!

Our Lives Can Go Off Course by Our Wrong Speaking

Maybe you haven't sinned like I did, but perhaps your mouth has been your undoing. The Book of James tells us clearly that our wrong talking can set the course of our life toward a destination we do not want to end up at.

James 3:4-5 NKJV

4 "Look also at ships: although they are so large and are driven by fierce winds, they are turned by a very small rudder wherever the pilot desires. 5 Even so the tongue is a little member and boasts great things."

See how great a forest a little fire kindles!

James 3:5 The Message

5 "A word out of your mouth may seem of no account, but it can accomplish nearly anything — or destroy it!"

YOU are the captain of the ship of YOUR LIFE. Your TONGUE, the words you say, is the RUDDER that DETERMINES what DIRECTION the ship goes, and ultimately, WHERE it will end up, and where your life will end up.

James also tells us that our tongue, our words are like the small spark that sets the whole forest on fire!

Jesus said you will HAVE whatever you BELIEVE and SAY (Mark 11:23). If you are not happy with what you HAVE, then perhaps you need to change what you are BELIEVING and SAYING.

Of course there can be other factors involved, in why your life hasn't turned out like you planned. Maybe other people's actions and decisions HAVE affected your life. Certainly that happens. We are going to deal with that later in this book, because the scripture gives us examples of that happening. And then of course, there is Satan, whose mission is to "steal, kill and destroy".

But the FIRST thing that we need to do is TAKE OWNERSHIP.

Let's take ownership for our lives, our decisions and our words. If we will get those lined up with the purpose and will of God, the devil can't stop us, nor can other people's actions stop us from having a blessed, purpose-filled life!

Now let's look again at Naomi...

Ruth 1:22 NKJV

22 "So Naomi returned, and Ruth the Moabitess, her daughter-in-law with her, who returned from the country of Moab. Now they came to Bethlehem at the beginning of the barley harvest."

The TIMING of when they returned was SIGNIFICANT, as we will see. They returned "at the beginning of the barley harvest." At that moment, Naomi did not realize how important the timing of her return was, but she was soon going to discover it.

Principle #4. Trust that God is ordering your steps, and working for your good.

When things haven't gone the way you planned it DOES NOT MEAN that God has forsaken or forgotten you! He is still working, as we will see. He was working for Naomi. God promises us, in the Book of Romans, that in ALL THINGS,

He is working for the good of those who love Him. Trust Him, He is working for your good! Even…and especially, when you can't see it!

Principle #5. Recognize the People and the Relationships That God Has Put Into Your Life.

As I have walked on this journey of restoration, I have come to appreciate more and more the people that God put in my life to encourage me, pray for me, give me wise counsel or just be a friend to me. Sometimes we just need a friend. I am grateful for those who stepped up to tell me they still believed in me and still loved me. They encouraged me that God has not given up on me, and neither have they. Thank God for folks like that in our lives.

God had given Ruth to Naomi. Her other daughter-in-law stayed in the land of Moab. But this is what Ruth said when Naomi tried to convince her to go back as well:

Ruth 1:16-17 NKJV

16 "But Ruth said: "Entreat me not to leave you, Or to turn back from following after you;

For wherever you go, I will go; And wherever you lodge, I will lodge; Your people shall be my people, And your God, my God. 17 Where you die, I will die, And there I will be buried.

The Lord do so to me, and more also, If anything but death parts you and me."

What a wonderful relationship! How great to have someone in your life, in this case a daughter-in-law, who says "I am with you for the rest of our lives, nothing but death will separate us." Wow!

Back to the narrative, Ruth and Nomi return to home, and it was at the beginning of the barley harvest. Ruth went out to glean in the fields. That's what the poor people did. God commanded the Israelites, that when they reaped their harvest, to leave behind the gleanings and what was growing in the corners of the field for the poor.

Ruth 2:3 NKJV

3 *"Then she left, and went and gleaned in the field after the reapers. And she happened to come to the part of the field belonging to Boaz, who was of the family of Elimelech."*

Ruth happened to go into Boaz's field. She went home and reported that news to Naomi:

Ruth 2:19-20 NKJV

19 *"And her mother-in-law said to her, "Where have you gleaned today? And where did you work? Blessed be the one who took notice of you." So she told her mother-in-law with whom she had worked, and said, "The man's name with whom I worked today is Boaz."*

20 *Then Naomi said to her daughter-in-law, "Blessed be he of the Lord, who has not forsaken His kindness to the living and*

the dead!" And Naomi said to her, "This man is a relation of ours, one of our close relatives."

A spark of hope returned to Naomi! God had not forsaken them after all! Boaz was not just a cousin, but a Kinsman-Redeemer. He would SIGNIFICANTLY change their financial situation and their future. If they had not come back at that season and time of the year during the barley harvest, it is highly unlikely that Ruth would have ever met Boaz.

God was working on Naomi's behalf, to restore what had been lost, to cause things to turn out well and for her to be blessed in the end. He was doing it through people that He had ALREADY placed in her life. One of them she had to RECOGNIZE and the other she had to RECONNECT with.

Ruth 2:22 NKJV

22 "And Naomi said to Ruth, her daughter-in-law, "It is good, my daughter, that you go out with his young women, and that people do not meet you in any other field."

Let me say this from observation. Through over 30 years of ministry I have seen people who bounce around from church to church, and then I have seen families who have stayed planted in the same church for many years. We need to be like Ruth and stay in the field where God leads us. We are going to be fed there. God connects us with the right people to bring about the recovery and restoration that we need in order to get our life back on course. He works through relationships, and by us being committed and faithful where He has planted us.

17

So Naomi advised Ruth on what to do to appeal to Boaz to be their "goel", which means their next of kin with certain family rights and duties…in other words, their Redeemer. Boaz took his role as kinsman redeemer and married Ruth. They had a baby, a grandson for Naomi. Being a grandparent myself, I can tell you that's about the greatest blessing that a person can have!

Ruth 4:14-15 NKJV

"Then the woman said to Naomi, "Blessed be the Lord, who has not left you this day without a close relative; and may his name be famous in Israel! 15 And may he be to you a restorer of life and a nourisher of your old age; for your daughter-in-law, who loves you, who is better to you than seven sons, has borne him."

It was said to Naomi about Ruth:

"Your daughter-in-law LOVES YOU, and she has been better to you than SEVEN SONS."

Notice the beginning part of the statement the women made to Naomi "Blessed be the Lord who has not left you." God has not left you! He is WITH you. He is FOR you!

Yes we may incur losses in our lives, but God can make it up to us in amazing ways! Naomi returned home after her losses as a very bitter woman, without hope. But God brought hope and new life and blessing back into her life. He can and will do the same for YOU!

3

THE STORY OF MOSES
When You Misinterpret
God's Plan

We probably have all faced, or may now be facing, times in our lives where it seems that life has not turned out like we planned. We had storybook ideals in our minds of living 'happily ever after'... and those hopes were dashed by a hard dose of reality.

Perhaps things didn't work out like you planned with your career and your financial situation. Or maybe you have experienced loss and dysfunction in your family relationships, maybe an unforeseen tragedy such as a premature death of a loved one.

Again the key question is, when that happens, what will we do? How will we respond?

In the next two chapters I want to look at two spiritual giants, Moses and Joseph. Each of these men came to a place in their life where life had not turned out like they planned.

In this chapter we will look at the life of Moses.

You are probably familiar with the story of Moses. He was born to Jewish parents, living in Egypt at a time when the Pharaoh ordered that all male babies among the Hebrews be put to death. His parents hid him after he was born in an attempt to spare his life, and by divine intervention he was discovered by Pharaoh's daughter, who took him in and raised him as her own son, with the aid of his actual mother who was hired to be his nurse!

Moses was destined by God to deliver the children of Israel from slavery in Egypt. He grew up as royalty, the son of Pharaoh's daughter, but when he reached the age of 40 that calling began to stir in him.

Acts 7:22-29 NKJV

22 "And Moses was learned in all the wisdom of the Egyptians, and was mighty in words and deeds. 23 Now when he was forty years old, it came into his heart to visit his brethren, the children of Israel. 24 And seeing one of them suffer wrong, he defended and avenged him who was oppressed, and struck down the Egyptian. 25 For he supposed that his brethren would have understood that God would deliver them by his hand, but they did not understand. 26 And the next day he appeared to two of them as they were fighting, and tried to reconcile them, saying, 'Men, you are brethren; why do you wrong one another?' 27 But he who did his neighbor wrong pushed him away, saying, 'Who made you a ruler and a judge over us? 28 Do you want to kill me as you did the Egyptian yesterday?' 29 Then, at this

saying, Moses fled and became a dweller in the land of Midian, where he had two sons."

For Moses, it looked like life had not turned out like he planned. He thought he had this calling on his life to deliver his people. But things went horribly wrong. In verse 25 in the above passage it stated *"He supposed that his brethren would have understood that God would deliver them by his hand, but they did not understand."*

Rather than thank him for showing up to deliver him, they defied his right to intervene in their lives. They did not recognize who he was or what he had been called to do to help them!

Maybe that has happened to you. Maybe God touched your heart to serve Him, you sensed a calling, had a desire, and began to take steps to pursue that calling. And perhaps, like Moses, the very people you felt called to help did not recognize nor appreciate the calling on your life. That can be a devastating realization. It seemed to be so for Moses.

Moses fled Egypt, and lived in the land of Midian for 40 years, trying to just survive and forget about the call of God on his life. But God was not finished with Moses. The call was still there, God still had a plan, even though Moses had misinterpreted that plan, and had attempted to bring it about in his own power.

Acts 7:30 NKJV

30 "And when forty years had passed, an Angel of the Lord appeared to him in a flame of fire in a bush, in the wilderness of Mount Sinai."

21

Forty years passed! Moses was now 80 years old. He'd been on medicare for 15 years already! Surely he was WAY TOO OLD to do anything meaningful for God, and certainly not on the scope of confronting the most powerful ruler on the earth, and leading millions of people out of slavery.

But God doesn't change His mind about His call on our lives, even though it seems that we have blown it. Look at this great promise from God concerning that:

Romans 11:29 The Message

29 "God's gifts and God's call are under full warranty — never canceled, never rescinded."

Sometimes Life Doesn't Turn Out Like We Planned Because We Misunderstand, or Misinterpret God's Call on Our Lives.

Moses first attempt to deliver the Israelites 40 years earlier was in his own power. Think about it, how far could he get, killing the Egyptians one by one? He could not have dreamed of what God had in mind, sending the mighty plagues of judgment that shook Egypt, and brought it to its knees.

So when God spoke to him from the burning bush, by that time Moses wanted nothing to do with that call. He felt like he had failed. In fact, he told God he couldn't do it because he couldn't speak well. But the scripture in Acts told us that he was mighty in word and deed. You can lose confidence in yourself after 40 years.

22

But God made His calling clear to Moses…

Exodus 3:10-11 NKJV

10 "Come now, therefore, and I will send you to Pharaoh that you may bring My people, the children of Israel, out of Egypt."

11 "But Moses said to God, "Who am I that I should go to Pharaoh, and that I should bring the children of Israel out of Egypt?"

Moses tried to make excuses and get out of his divine assignment. He suggested that the Lord find someone else to do the job. Surely there were others more qualified than I, he reasoned.

Exodus 4:13 NKJV

13 "But he said, 'O my Lord, please send by the hand of whomever else You may send.'"

Finally, after all the excuses, and protests and pleas to find someone else to do it, Moses obeyed and headed down to Egypt. And God was with him.

You know the rest of the story, he and Aaron confronted Pharaoh, the ten plagues were visited on the land of Egypt, and the Israelites finally went free. They had the miracle of the parting of the Red Sea for the final act of their deliverance, and defeated Pharaoh and the Egyptian army, and then for the next 40 years Moses led the nation of Israel toward the promised land.

Here are a few highlights from Moses life:

He went up on the mountain and met with God, and received the 10 Commandments.

He wrote the first five books of the Bible!

God performed many signs and wonders through his hands.

Today, nearly 3,500 years later, Moses is known and recognized, rightly so, as one of the greatest men to ever walk the earth.

So what can we learn from Moses?

Don't try to fulfill God's call in your own ability.

Seek to understand God's call on your life, don't misinterpret it.

But if you have tried to fulfill God's call in your own strength, and have fallen flat, or if you have misinterpreted God's calling on your life, it's not too late! God is bigger than that!

Even if you feel broken, defeated and powerless, God can still use you! And His plan and call on your life will be fulfilled IF you will follow Him.

No, things might not have turned out as you originally envisioned them, but God can and will use your life for His glory if you will surrender it to Him, follow Him in faith and obedience, and trust His goodness.

David, who certainly made many mistakes in his life, proclaimed in the 23rd Psalm that "Goodness and mercy shall follow me ALL THE DAYS of my life." That was not just for David. That is for YOU! The Lord is YOUR SHEPHERD too! Believe that goodness and mercy from God are following you TODAY! Believe that God is working to restore your life and set you back on the track of His calling and purpose for your life.

4

THE STORY OF JOSEPH
When Others Have
Betrayed You

Maybe you have experienced betrayal from others. Perhaps your life has taken a terrible and tragic turn because of the harmful actions of others. It can happen. We live in a fallen world, where life is not fair, and can in fact, be cruel. What do you do, how can you recover, when things have turned out like this for you?

We see this principle illustrated in the life of Joseph. Joseph was the 11th son of Jacob, born to him through his wife Rachel. He was a favored son, he was given a "coat of many colors" that marked him as the favored son. As a result, his brothers were jealous of him and hated him.

As a teenager, Joseph had a dream, in which it revealed that his brothers would bow down to him and serve him. He made the mistake of telling the dream to his brothers, and they hated him even more!

27

The dream was FROM GOD! It was regarding the future!

But things went horribly wrong for Joseph. His brothers sold him to Midianite traders who took him to Egypt, and he was sold in the slave market there to a man named Potiphar.

God's hand was on Joseph, and even though he was in slavery God caused him to prosper and blessed the whole house of Potiphar because of Joseph.

We know that Joseph served and followed God, and lived with integrity through that trying ordeal, because when Potiphar's wife tried to seduce him, here is how he responded:

Genesis 39:8-9 NKJV

8 *"But he refused and said to his master's wife, "Look, my master does not know what is with me in the house, and he has committed all that he has to my hand. 9 There is no one greater in this house than I, nor has he kept back anything from me but you, because you are his wife. How then can I do this great wickedness, and sin against God?"*

Lesser men would have yielded to that temptation, justifying it in fact by saying, "Look at what God has let happen to me, why should I try to live right?"

But Joseph didn't do that, he rejected her advances, and as a result he was falsely accused by Potiphar's wife, and ended up in prison!

And surely in that prison, where he stayed for several years (he was 17 when he was sold into slavery and was 30 when he came out of prison) he had to think "My life certainly did not turn out like I planned." No doubt his dreams of greatness became nightmares that mocked him day after day.

Incredibly, Joseph maintained a good attitude, and the blessing and favor of God was evident in his life. God's blessing and favor can be over your life, but if you live with a bad attitude, you will short-circuit that blessing and favor.

Genesis 39:21-23 NKJV

21 "But the Lord was with Joseph and showed him mercy, and He gave him favor in the sight of the keeper of the prison. 22 And the keeper of the prison committed to Joseph's hand all the prisoners who were in the prison; whatever they did there, it was his doing. 23 The keeper of the prison did not look into anything that was under Joseph's authority, because the Lord was with him; and whatever he did, the Lord made it prosper."

Even if you find yourself in the most adverse, uncomfortable and unjust of situations, if you will keep a right heart toward God, and not get bitter or negative, God will cause you to be blessed and prosper!

Eventually, two of Pharaoh's prominent servants came to be prisoners. They had dreams and Joseph interpreted them. One servant was going to be executed, but the other was going to be restored. Joseph told him his story and said please remember me to Pharaoh. But once the servant was restored, he forgot about Joseph. For two years...

Can you imagine the disappointment? Joseph was waiting day after day, hoping to hear some good news about his release, and two years passed.

Sometimes there are people we are counting on to help us, and they are in a position to help us, but they forget, or they don't for whatever reason. We have to keep our eyes on God, and our hope in Him and not get bitter for others' failure to help us.

Finally, after two years, Pharaoh had two dreams that were vivid and very troubling. He called in the magicians and wise men of Egypt, but they could not interpret the dreams. As his servant, who had been in prison with Joseph, heard the dreams, and the dilemma of Pharaoh to find someone to tell him the meaning, he suddenly remembered – Joseph!

Genesis 41:14 NKJV

14 *"Then Pharaoh sent and called Joseph, and they brought him quickly out of the dungeon; and he shaved, changed his clothing, and came to Pharaoh."*

Joseph didn't have to take a crash course, he was READY. He had been faithfully following God, faithfully using the gifts God had given him, and he never gave up on the dreams God had given him.

If he had allowed bitterness to fester in his heart, if he had gotten mad at God and not maintained his integrity and obedience to God, when it seemed that it was all in vain, he would not have had the clarity in his spirit to hear from God, and accurately interpret Pharaoh's dreams.

39 "Then Pharaoh said to Joseph, "Inasmuch as God has shown you all this, there is no one as discerning and wise as you. 40 You shall be over my house, and all my people shall be ruled according to your word; only in regard to the throne will I be greater than you." 41 And Pharaoh said to Joseph, "See, I have set you over all the land of Egypt."

Joseph was READY when his hour of opportunity, favor and exaltation came. He went from living in prison, to living in the palace, and he was second in command over the whole nation of Egypt in ONE DAY!

In another sense, it was much longer than one day. It was all those years of staying faithful to God, continuing to trust God and not allowing himself to give up or get bitter. All of those things were preparing Joseph for that day when he went from the prison to the palace. And he was ready!

And so the prophetic dream came to pass after all. Seven years of plenty, followed by seven years of severe famine. And one day, two years into the famine, Joseph's brothers showed up to buy grain and yes, they bowed down to the most powerful man in Egypt, their brother Joseph, just as Joseph had seen in his dreams years earlier.

But instead of exacting revenge, Joseph forgave them, opening the way for a wonderful family restoration and reunion!

Genesis 45:3-5 NKJV

3 "Then Joseph said to his brothers, "I am Joseph; does my father still live?" But his brothers could not answer him, for they were dismayed in his presence. 4 And Joseph said to his brothers, "Please come near to me." So they came near. Then he said: "I am Joseph your brother, whom you sold into Egypt. 5 But now, do not therefore be grieved or angry with yourselves because you sold me here; for God sent me before you to preserve life."

Joseph revealed the secret of how he had been able to keep his heart right, his attitude right, and not give up on his dreams, or on God.

He Was Able to See the Hand of God at Work, Even Through the Actions of Those Who Sought to Do Him Harm!

Genesis 50:19-20 NKJV

19 "Joseph said to them, "Do not be afraid, for am I in the place of God? 20 But as for you, you meant evil against me; but God meant it for good, in order to bring it about as it is this day, to save many people alive."

Here is another divine principle of recovery when life has gone wrong:

Forgive, and Trust that God Can Work, Even Through Those Who Have Betrayed or Harmed You.

If Joseph had appointed himself judge, jury and executioner of his brothers, he would have been putting himself in the place of

32

God. This is not to say that we excuse, ignore or fail to protect ourselves from abusive relationships, but for our own sakes we must FORGIVE, and not allow the harm that has been done to us to be compounded by getting bitter and vengeful ourselves.

God will cause you to rise above every evil perpetrated against you if you will call out to Him, trust in Him, and continue to live with integrity and honor. Though it seems your dreams have been crushed and there is no hope of your life turning out like you had planned or dreamed, God can turn things around in an amazing way, yes even sometimes overnight, and bring you into a glorious and blessed future!

5

WHAT TO DO WHEN SATAN ATTACKS

Sometimes, when life doesn't turn out like we planned, we can trace the root cause to an outright direct attack from Satan. Sure, he is involved when our own actions cause our life to get off course, through temptation and deception. Certainly he is the motivation behind others who have betrayed or harmed us. But there are times when his attacks are even more direct, more forceful. As we see in the story of Job…

The Story of Job:

Job 1:1-3 NKJV

"There was a man in the land of Uz, whose name was Job; and that man was blameless and upright, and one who feared God and shunned evil. 2 And seven sons and three daughters were born to him. 3 Also, his possessions were seven thousand sheep, three thousand camels, five hundred yoke of oxen, five hundred female donkeys, and a very large household, so that this man was the greatest of all the people of the East."

Job's life was good! He was a righteous man, he feared God, shunned evil. He was blessed with 10 children. He was very, very wealthy. The devil hates the righteous. And he certainly hates the *wealthy* righteous! So he set out to attack Job.

Satan approached the Throne of God, to get a judgment against Job:

Job 1:8 NKJV

8 "Then the Lord said to Satan, "Have you considered My servant Job, that there is none like him on the earth, a blameless and upright man, one who fears God and shuns evil?"

Let me clear up a misconception here. God was not pointing Job out to Satan, as if to say "Hey, why don't come over and attack him." The literal Hebrew here for the word "considered" is – *set your heart on*. The Lord recognized that Satan had already noticed Job, and how God had blessed him, and that Satan had already set his heart on attacking him.

Jesus made it clear that this is indeed Satan's mode of operation.

John 10:10 NKJV

10 "The thief does not come except to steal, and to kill, and to destroy"…

Satan's ONLY motive in setting his heart on Job, was to steal, kill and destroy him. Satan then made an interesting observation about Job, that was TRUE, and that can be true in our lives today:

Job 1:10 NLT

10 "You have always put a wall of protection around him and his home (household) and his property. You have made him prosper in everything he does. Look how rich he is!"

A casual reading of the story of Job has caused people to think that God decided just to arbitrarily lift His hand of protection from Job. But that was not the case. We get insight into why and how Satan was able to breach the "wall of protection" that God had placed around Job in the following scripture:

Job 3:25 NKJV

25 "For the thing I greatly feared has come upon me,

And what I dreaded has happened to me."

The wall of protection had gaps in it, because Job was living in fear and worry. The Bible speaks of the SHIELD of FAITH. Fear and worry are opposite of faith. When we are in fear and worry, we have laid down the shield of faith, and are susceptible to Satan's fiery darts. In Job's case, Satan had the opening that he needed. And literally all hell breaks loose in Job's life.

Job 1:13-19 NKJV

13 "Now there was a day when his sons and daughters were eating and drinking wine in their oldest brother's house; 14 and a messenger came to Job and said, "The oxen were plowing and the donkeys feeding beside them, 15 when the Sabeans raided them and took them away — indeed they have killed the servants with the edge of the sword; and I alone have escaped to tell you!" 16 While he was still speaking, another also came and said, "The fire of God fell from heaven and burned up the sheep and the servants, and consumed them; and I alone have escaped to tell you!" 17 While he was still speaking, another also came and said, "The Chaldeans formed three bands, raided the camels and took them away, yes, and killed the servants with the edge of the sword; and I alone have escaped to tell you!" 18 While he was still speaking, another also came and said, "Your sons and daughters were eating and drinking wine in their oldest brother's house, 19 and suddenly a great wind came from across the wilderness and struck the four corners of the house, and it fell on the young people, and they are dead; and I alone have escaped to tell you!"

Talk About a Bad Day!!!

Notice the phrase that is repeated "while he was still speaking". Apparently all of those major tragedies struck Job in ONE DAY! I dare say that none of us has ever experienced a "bad day" on the order of what Job did that day. This was a direct onslaught of Satan.

Satan attacked Job's Character.

Satan attacked Job's Possessions.

Satan attacked Job's Family.

Satan attacked Job's Health.

These are the same areas he will try to attack us in. After it all happened, Job attempted to stay true to God, and as far as he knew, he was. But he was lacking in insight.

Job 1:21 NKJV

21 "And he said:

"Naked I came from my mother's womb,

And naked shall I return there.

The Lord gave, and the Lord has taken away;

Blessed be the name of the Lord."

Wait a minute! The Lord had given, YES. But was it the Lord who had taken away?

Job could not see or hear what was happening at the Court of Heaven. He did not know it was the devil that was behind what was happening to him.

I was watching intently this past September, as our nation remembered 9/11 and they replayed the video of the attacks, and the news commentary. We look back now, and we know the second plane is going to hit the South Tower, we know the plane is going to hit the Pentagon, we know the Towers are going to fall, we know United 93 is going to be taken over by the crew and crash in Shanksville, PA. But in the moment, as it was unfolding, none of us knew what was coming next, or the scope of what was really happening.

And in the middle of what was happening to him, Job didn't know it was the devil. There is very little revelation of Satan and his works in the Old Testament.

The bulk of the Book of Job, from chapter two through chapter thirty-seven, consists of Job's friends telling him there must be sin in his life that he has done well to conceal, for this to be happening to him. Job maintained his innocence. Then God showed up...and said "Let me ask you some questions..." After the Divine interrogation, Job replied...

Job 42:3 NKJV

3 "You asked, 'Who is this who hides counsel without knowledge?'

Therefore I have uttered what I did not understand,

Things too wonderful for me, which I did not know."

Job realized he was talking about things, making assertions about God, things that he knew NOTHING about. Job is not alone in doing that, by the way. Well-meaning people, even theologians, have been doing that in every generation since Job. Another revealing statement made by Job, as his life is about to go into recovery mode is this:

Job 42:5-6 NKJV

5 "I have heard of You by the hearing of the ear,

But now my eye sees You.

6 Therefore I abhor myself,

And repent in dust and ashes."

A lot of people have said things about God, because they heard someone say something, and some can say it with authority and sound convincing. But they haven't really SEEN HIM, haven't gotten to know His character and nature.

So Job repented, and at God's direction Job prayed for his friends, because they were REALLY in trouble with God for saying what they had said. Then we read this...

Job 42:10 NKJV

10 "And the Lord restored Job's losses when he prayed for his friends. Indeed the Lord gave Job twice as much as he had before."

It obviously took some time for all this to come to pass and for everything in Job's life to be restored, but it happened! And God restored to Job twice as much as he had before!

Job 42:16-17 NKJV

16 "After this Job lived one hundred and forty years, and saw his children and grandchildren for four generations. 17 So Job died, old and full of days."

He lived happily ever after.

I want to point out four truths that will help you to recover when Satan has attacked you.

#1. Recognize There IS a Devil – And He is the One Attacking You, Not God

We can't blame everything on the devil, but yet we do need to recognize when he is at work, so that we can deal with him. Jesus identified Satan as the culprit in this passage from the Gospel of Luke:

Luke 13:10-13

10 "Now He was teaching in one of the synagogues on the Sabbath. 11 And behold, there was a woman who had a spirit of infirmity eighteen years, and was bent over and could in no way raise herself up. 12 But when Jesus saw her, He called her to Him and said to her, "Woman, you are loosed from your infirmity." 13 And He laid His hands on her, and immediately she was made straight, and glorified God."

Notice the scripture says that this woman was bound "with a spirit of infirmity". Her condition was the direct result of a satanic attack. Later in the passage, Jesus reaffirms that truth.

Luke 13:16

16 "So ought not this woman, being a daughter of Abraham, whom Satan has bound — think of it — for eighteen years, be loosed from this bond on the Sabbath?"

Satan was the one who had bound her. He was to blame, not God. And Jesus came into the Synagogue that day and set the woman free from the Satanic oppression that had bound her.

#2. Make Sure You Have Not Let Gaps Come into God's Hedge Around You

As mentioned earlier in this chapter, fear and worry can create gaps in our hedge of protection. Another thing that will open our lives to Satan's attack is willful disobedience to God's Word or will for your life.

1 Peter 5:8-9

8 "Be sober, be vigilant; because your adversary the devil walks about like a roaring lion, seeking whom he may devour. 9 Resist him, steadfast in the faith, knowing that the same sufferings are experienced by your brotherhood in the world."

Notice that Satan is "seeking whom he MAY devour". Our permission, our cooperation is necessary. Many times people are unaware that they are granting Satan access and permission into their lives. Satan can attack you at random, but he cannot devour you without your PERMISSION!

What are we to do? Peter says in verse 9…"resist him"…

#3. Resist Him, Steadfast in the Faith!

Use the authority of the Name of Jesus! Command Satan to take his hands off of your finances, your family, and your body. Be steadfast in FAITH. Believe God's Word over the circumstances. Hold on to the promises of God, by holding fast your confession of faith!

James 4:7 NKJV

7 "Therefore submit to God. Resist the devil and he will flee from you."

You "submit to God" by obeying His Word. Then you are in a position to resist the devil, and he will FLEE FROM YOU!

Paul and the Messenger of Satan

The Apostle Paul speaks of encountering Satanic opposition as he endeavored to spread the Gospel of Jesus Christ to the known world in his day.

2 Corinthians 12:7 NKJV

7 "And lest I should be exalted above measure by the abundance of the revelations, a thorn in the flesh was given to me, a messenger of Satan to buffet me, lest I be exalted above measure."

He speaks of a "thorn in the flesh" which he identified as "a messenger of Satan" that was sent to "buffet him" or deal blow after blow in a continual, persistent and ongoing attack.

2 Corinthians 12:7 God's Word

"I am forced to deal with a recurring problem. That problem, Satan's messenger"...

First of all, what was Paul doing?

Carrying the Gospel throughout the Mediterranean region, writing 13 or 14 books of the New Testament. Proclaiming the great truths of redemption that Jesus had revealed to him. Do you think the devil wanted to stop him?

Everywhere Paul went, the devil, this messenger of Satan, would show up, to stir up trouble, try to stop Paul, for the purpose of hindering the spread of the Gospel.

1 Thessalonians 2:18 NKJV

18 "Therefore we wanted to come to you — even I, Paul, time and again — but Satan hindered us."

Notice what he did NOT say. He did not say "everything happens for a reason, I guess God didn't want us to come." No, he recognized that Satan was attempting to hinder him.

So what happened?

2 Corinthians 12:8-9 NKJV

8 "Concerning this thing I pleaded with the Lord three times that it might depart from me. 9 And He said to me, "My grace is sufficient for you, for My strength is made perfect in weakness. "...

In essence, Paul was asking "Lord will you get rid of the devil so I don't have to deal with him?"

What was Jesus' response to Paul and to US? "My grace is sufficient for you, My power is made perfect in weakness."

(that is when we acknowledge our weakness, and recognize we must depend on the Lord).

I want to point out that this is in no way a resignation to defeat!

2 Corinthians 12:9-10 NKJV

... *"Therefore most gladly I will rather boast in my infirmities, that the power of Christ may rest upon me. 10 Therefore I take pleasure in infirmities, in reproaches, in needs, in persecutions, in distresses, for Christ's sake. For when I am weak, then I am strong."*

What was the thorn? Paul identifies it here. Infirmities, which means weaknesses (in Romans 8 we are told that the Holy Spirit helps us in our infirmities in regard to prayer). Paul goes on to list Reproaches, Needs, Persecutions, Distresses. The messenger of Satan was producing these negative things in Paul's life. But after Paul learned the secret to victory, he was no longer frustrated and depressed by these things, but said that he could now "boast in my infirmities". He could do so, knowing that the power of Christ would rest upon him.

#4. Understand That God's Grace Upon You is Sufficient to Overcome Every Attack of the Devil

Did the Devil Win? Was the Messenger of Satan successful over Paul? Let's see what Paul says...

2 Corinthians 2:14 NKJV

14 "Now thanks be to God who always leads us in triumph in Christ, and through us diffuses the fragrance of His knowledge in every place. "

2 Timothy 4:7 NKJV

7 "I have fought the good fight, I have finished the race, I have kept the faith. "

Paul wrote thirteen of the twenty-seven books in the New Testament, fourteen if we include the Book of Hebrews, which many scholars attribute to Paul. He wrote them as letters to the various churches of that day. We hold those letters in our hands even now. We read them today and they give us faith. We read them today and we understand who we are in Christ. We read them today and know our authority over the devil! No, the messenger of Satan did not succeed! Paul was indeed more than a conqueror! And his life is an example to us, that no attack of Satan can stop us from fulfilling the purpose of God for our lives if we will trust in God's grace, and allow the power of Christ to rest upon us!

6

WHAT TO DO WHEN YOU DON'T KNOW WHAT TO DO

You woke up one day, and your life came crashing down all around you. Maybe it was a sudden tragedy, or perhaps it was the culmination of years of bad decisions, self-neglect, or a combination of many factors. The bottom line though, is that your life has not turned out like you planned. As you begin the process to rebuild and restore your life, there will be times where you simply don't know WHAT to do. The devastation seems so widespread and overwhelming you don't even know where to begin the clean-up process. What do you do, when you don't know what to do??? Believe it or not, we have examples of this in the Word of God, to inspire us and to give us faith.

King Jehoshaphat and the People of Judah

2 Chronicles 20:1-4 NKJV

"It happened after this that the people of Moab with the people of Ammon, and others with them besides the Ammonites, came to battle against Jehoshaphat. 2 Then some came and told

Jehoshaphat, saying, "A great multitude is coming against you from beyond the sea, from Syria; and they are in Hazazon Tamar" (which is En Gedi). 3 And Jehoshaphat feared, and set himself to seek the Lord, and proclaimed a fast throughout all Judah. 4 So Judah gathered together to ask help from the Lord; and from all the cities of Judah they came to seek the Lord."

King Jehoshaphat leads the nation in prayer, and concludes his prayer with these words...

2 Chronicles 20:12 NKJV

12 "O our God, will You not judge them? For we have no power against this great multitude that is coming against us; nor do we know what to do, but our eyes are upon You."

King Jehoshaphat and the people of Judah were facing an attack of overwhelming proportions.

Three enemy armies had come together to attack Judah, destroy them and take their land. Jehoshaphat admitted to God in prayer "we don't know what to do".

But he had already acted wisely. He had assembled the people together to look to the Lord for an answer.

What do we do when faced with a situation that we don't know what to do? This account from scripture gives us principles that we can apply in our lives today.

#1. Ask Help From the Lord

We "have not" because we "ask not". God WANTS to help us, but we have to ASK. Prayer gives God an INVITATION to work on our behalf.

#2. Seek the Lord

This is not the same as asking for help. In asking help you are TELLING God your need.

In seeking the Lord you are awaiting, listening for His guidance, His wisdom, His solution.

#3. Keep Your Eyes on Him

Jehoshaphat said "our eyes are upon You". That's a nice statement, but just HOW do we do that?

Have you ever seen God? Physically? Most of us have not. We keep our EYES on Him by looking to His Word, His Promise.

They could have easily turned their eyes to see the vast multitude coming against them, and panicked. But they were determined to keep their eyes on the Lord, on His promise and on the Covenant that they had with Him.

Remember when Peter walked on the water?

As long as Peter looked upon Jesus he was doing fine, even though the wind and waves were raging all around him. When he turned his gaze from Jesus (the Word) to notice the wind and waves, he was AFRAID and began to sink.

When you don't know what to do, keep your eyes on God, by keeping your eyes on the Word of God. Keep doing what you KNOW to do, from God's Word!——

If your finances are under attack DON'T STOP tithing! Keep doing the Word!

Keep reading the Word daily. That's where your answer is going to come from. That's what's going to keep your faith strong! This is what brought me through the darkest times of my life when my world had crashed in around me. As I read the scriptures, in desperation really, God mercifully, powerfully spoke to me His promises of restoration and healing!

As the people of Judah gathered together, seeking the Lord, the Spirit came upon one of them, and he prophesied these most important words to them, and to YOU today!

2 Chronicles 20:15 NKJV

15 "And he said, "Listen, all you of Judah and you inhabitants of Jerusalem, and you, King Jehoshaphat! Thus says the Lord to you: 'Do not be afraid nor dismayed because of this great multitude, for the battle is not yours, but God's."

#4. Don't Be Afraid or Dismayed, the Battle Belongs to God!

The devil wants to get you to fear, to panic and be dismayed. Then you really will make the wrong decision and do the wrong thing, falling right into the trap Satan has set for you.

Do we truly believe that God will fight our battles for us? Do we truly believe He loves us that much? The people of Israel were His servants. We are His sons and daughters!

In the case of Jehoshaphat and Judah, God spoke to them, told them what to do, they obeyed, and then they did something quite remarkable:

2 Chronicles 20:20 NKJV

20 "So they rose early in the morning (that would be remarkable for some) and went out into the Wilderness of Tekoa; and as they went out, Jehoshaphat stood and said, "Hear me, O Judah and you inhabitants of Jerusalem: Believe in the Lord your God, and you shall be established; believe His prophets, and you shall prosper."

Believe in the Lord and you shall be established.

The New Living Translation says *"you will be able to STAND FIRM."*

It was critical that they be established and that they stand firm. When you can't see a way out of your adverse circumstances, it is critical that you become established in the fact that God loves you, He is for you, He wants to help you, and He will sustain and deliver you, as you put your trust in Him.

2 Chronicles 20:21 NKJV

21 "And when he had consulted with the people, he appointed those who should sing to the Lord, and who should praise the beauty of holiness, as they went out before the army and were saying: "Praise the Lord, For His mercy endures forever."

#5. When You Don't Know What to Do – Praise God!

2 Chronicles 20:22 NKJV

22 *"Now when they began to sing and to praise, the Lord set ambushes against the people of Ammon, Moab, and Mount Seir, who had come against Judah; and they were defeated."*

Praise Him because He is good!

Praise Him because His mercy endures forever!

When we praise Him, He comes on the scene in our situation!

I know it sounds simple. I know you have heard it before, it is the DOER of the Word that is blessed, not just the HEARER.

When the people of Judah began to sing and praise THEN God went to work to confuse and defeat the enemy. Our praise, heart-felt and OUT LOUD, releases God to work on our behalf like nothing else can.

When you don't know what to do, begin to praise God! One thing that will happen is that your praise will silence the voices of doubt, fear and defeat that are coming against your mind. We are told in the Book of Psalms that praise, even the praise from an infant, will "silence the enemy and the avenger".

#6. Pray Expecting God to Answer and Show You What to Do

Jeremiah 33:3 NKJV

3 "Call to Me, and I will answer you, and show you great and mighty things, which you do not know."

In the margin of my Bible, for the word mighty, it says "inaccessible".

When we pray, we access what is otherwise inaccessible, what can be accessed no other way, except by prayer.

Yeah that sounds good and all but I don't even know what to pray for! I'm so glad you brought that up! God has given us a way to pray, when we don't know what to pray for!

Romans 8:26 NKJV

*26 "Likewise the Spirit also helps in our weaknesses. **For we do not know what we should pray for as we ought**, but the Spirit Himself makes intercession for us with groanings which cannot be uttered."*

As noted linguist and Greek scholar P.C. Nelson pointed out this "groaning" includes praying in other tongues. As we pray in tongues, we are able to pray about things that our mind cannot yet grasp. Why, because we are praying out of our spirit, by the help of the Holy Spirit.

Romans 8:27 NKJV

27 "Now He who searches the hearts knows what the mind of the Spirit is, because He makes intercession for the saints according to the will of God."

When we pray in tongues we are praying the perfect will of God!

1 Corinthians 14:2 NKJV

"For he who speaks in a tongue does not speak to men but to God, for no one understands him; however, in the spirit he speaks mysteries."

The word "mysteries" can also be interpreted as "divine secrets". By praying in the spirit, you are able to go beyond your own understanding, and pray the perfect will of God over your situation, and ask God to do things that your mind doesn't even know need to be done!!!

#7. Pray Out Your Answer by Praying in Tongues

Romans 8:28 NKJV

28 "And we know that all things work together for good to those who love God, to those who are called according to His purpose."

This is not some random thought. Paul did not have a chapter template and was trying to find something to fit into the verse 28 slot! It is connected to what he said in the previous verses…

Romans 8:26-27

26 "Likewise the Spirit also helps in our weaknesses. For we do not know what we should pray for as we ought, but the Spirit Himself makes intercession for us with groanings which cannot be uttered. 27 Now He who searches the hearts knows what the mind of the Spirit is, because He makes intercession for the saints according to the will of God."

We don't know what to pray for as we ought. But we have a Helper, the Holy Spirit! If we will yield to Him, and pray in the Spirit, we are praying out the perfect will of God, even if we don't have understanding in our minds.

And THEN, we can TRUST that ALL THINGS ARE WORKING TOGETHER FOR OUR GOOD!!!

#8. Follow the Peace of God

Colossians 3:15

15 "And let the peace of God rule in your hearts, to which also you were called in one body; and be thankful."

Colossians 3:15 Amplified Bible, Classic Edition

[15] *"And let the peace (soul harmony which comes) from Christ rule (act as umpire continually) in your hearts [deciding and settling with finality all questions that arise in your minds"*...

Let peace rule in your heart. What brings you peace? Which choice, what course of action, brings you peace? God has given us His peace. If we will be led by that peace we will know what

57

to do, what steps to take, and what decisions to make that will lead us out of despair, devastation and defeat, and into a place of victory, joy and restoration!

7

THE MAN OF GOD IN THE FILTHY CLOTHES

As I mentioned in chapter one, after my world came crashing down, I cried out to the Lord and in His mercy He answered me, and began to remind me of promises in His word. I remember very clearly, as I was a couple of months into the process of restoration, I kept hearing in my spirit "read the scripture about the man of God in filthy clothes". That prompting persisted for a couple of days until I finally took time to find the passage of scripture that I knew the Holy Spirit was referring to. I knew it was the book of Zechariah, and I found it in chapter three…

Zechariah 3:1-3 NLT

"Then the angel showed me Jeshua the high priest standing before the angel of the Lord. The Accuser, Satan, was there at the angel's right hand, making accusations against Jeshua. 2 And the Lord said to Satan, "I, the Lord, reject your accusations, Satan. Yes, the Lord, who has chosen Jerusalem, rebukes you.

This man is like a burning stick that has been snatched from the fire."

3 "Jeshua's clothing was filthy as he stood there before the angel."

Jeshua (or Joshua in other translations) was the High Priest. Zechariah was granted access to see what was happening to Jeshua in the realm of the spirit. He was in the Court of Heaven, and Satan was making accusations against him. Zechariah also saw that Jeshua was clothed with filthy garments. As we read on in the passage we see that this represented sin in Jeshua's life, that Satan was using to accuse and condemn him.

Zechariah 3:4 NLT

4 "So the angel said to the others standing there, "Take off his filthy clothes." And turning to Jeshua he said, "See, I have taken away your sins, and now I am giving you these fine new clothes."

Something wonderful takes place here, that the Lord wanted me to see, and perhaps you need to see for your situation. First of all, the Lord speaks, with great power and authority "I the Lord reject your accusations Satan!" This spoke so powerfully to me during that season when I was battling so much shame and guilt. Satan was hurling accusing thoughts at me continually, but the Lord REJECTED those accusations, and I knew He wanted me to reject them too!

I love the way it reads in God's Word translation:

Zechariah 3:2 God's Word

2 "The Lord said to Satan, "I, the Lord, silence you, Satan! I, the Lord, who has chosen Jerusalem, silence you!"

The Lord wants you to know that He can SILENCE the accusations that Satan is making against you and me. When we repent of our sin, and apply the cleansing blood of Jesus over our lives, Satan has no legal right to condemn, accuse or shame us!

As Jeshua stands there, before the Lord, the Angel issues an order "take off his filthy clothes". And then he says to Jeshua "see, I have taken away your sins." The filthy clothes represented the sin in his life, which the LORD REMOVED. Then he is told "I am giving you these fine new clothes!"

God clothes us in His righteousness when we come to Him for salvation, and when we RETURN to Him in repentance. Zechariah watches this amazing scene unfold before him, then he speaks up...

Zechariah 3:5 NLT

5 "Then I said, "They should also place a clean turban on his head." So they put a clean priestly turban on his head and dressed him in new clothes while the angel of the Lord stood by."

Of course the turban for the head of Jeshua represents his THOUGHT LIFE. To walk free from the guilt and shame of the past we must change our thinking, and begin to think God's

61

thoughts about ourselves. The process continues for Jeshua until he is clothed fully in the new clothing.

Next, Jeshua (Joshua) is given a directive and a promise from the Lord...

Zechariah 3:6-7 NKJV

6 *"Then the Angel of the Lord admonished Joshua, saying, 7 "Thus says the Lord of hosts:*

'If you will walk in My ways, And if you will keep My command, Then you shall also judge My house, And likewise have charge of My courts; I will give you places to walk

Among those who stand here."

I knew this was the Lord speaking to me as well, concerning future ministry, which at the time I thought was probably over. The Lord was telling me that if I would walk in His ways, and keep His word, that He would restore spiritual authority to me, and that I would walk in the spirit in a greater measure than I ever had before.

An amazing experience:

Of course I held on to this promise and would read and pray this passage over my life regularly. Eleven months after the Lord first led me to this scripture, I had a most remarkable experience in fulfillment of the promise. I had resumed teaching and preaching by this time, and one Sunday morning, during our praise and worship, as I was standing by my seat on the front row, before I went to the platform to minister I had a strange sensation. I actually felt like I was wearing a heavy coat. I knew I had a sports coat on, and it was cool weather outside, so I thought "Did I forget to take my overcoat off?" I reached my hand up and felt, and it was just my sport coat, but it felt much heavier.

Then I remembered the scripture, and how God had spoken to me eleven months before "I am giving you these fine new clothes." I understood that He was anointing me with a new anointing, restoring what had been lost, to an even greater degree.

Right now it may seem your life has not turned out like you planned. God wants to restore you! He wants to take off the filthy clothes of sin, guilt and shame, silence the accusing voice of Satan, and clothe you with new clothes, of righteousness, joy and His anointing!

8

FINAL WORDS OF ENCOURAGEMENT

At the time of this writing, it has been seven years since the day my world came crashing down, and I thought my life was over. Just as an athlete who has been injured has to take time away from the sport he plays in order to heal, I had to take time away from the constant demands of the ministry. I needed to be healed myself, not physically, but in my soul. I desperately wanted to see my marriage and family restored, but I knew the first place I had to focus on was what was going on inside of me.

As I mentioned in Chapter One, the Lord began to speak to me through His word, giving me promises that began to restore hope and bring healing to my soul. In the midst of my brokenness He began to restore my soul. A few dear friends stood with me through those days, and without their prayers and encouragement I would not have made it. I am grateful to the Lord for placing them in my life, and for giving them the grace to walk with me, and still believe in me and encourage me.

Now, seven years later, I can attest to the fact that God has brought wonderful restoration in many areas in my life. The restoration process is not complete, but I can truly say that God has been faithful! There certainly have been days that I have been discouraged, that I have wanted to give up, and I suspect that you will have those days too. But I knew enough to just stay steady, to not give up, and I can tell you I have come through each of those dark, discouraging days, to see many blessings and good things that I would have missed if I had quit. So don't you dare quit!

One of the things that has been key for my healing and restoration, once I had healed sufficiently to do so, was to begin to share with others, and encourage them using my story and the scriptures. Part of that, for me, meant going in to share with the inmates at the county jail. What a fitting message for them –"What to Do When Life Doesn't Turn Out Like You Planned."

It is my hope and prayer that my story, and the examples from the Bible that I have shared in this book have encouraged and enlightened you, and have strengthened your faith. God is no respecter of persons. That means that He will do for you what He has done for others. He loves you greatly! He has an amazing plan for your life! No matter where you are or what you have done, it's not too late to give your life to Him fully and completely, and let Him turn it around and bring beauty from the ashes!

Appendix: Scriptures of Restoration

Here are some of the scriptures the Lord guided me to, that facilitated His work of restoration in my life. I pray that they will inspire and encourage you as well!

Isaiah 57:17-18 NKJV

For the iniquity of his covetousness
I was angry and struck him; I hid and was angry,
And he went on backsliding in the way of his heart.
18 I have seen his ways, and will heal him;
I will also lead him, and restore comforts to him and to his mourners.

This was the one of the first verses that the Lord led me to. It described my situation clearly, but then gave me a wonderful promise to hold onto. God said that He had seen my ways, my sin, but in His mercy, He said that He would HEAL me and also LEAD me, and then restore comforts to me and to my mourners (those I had hurt because of my sin).

Psalms 27:13-14 NKJV

13 I would have lost heart, unless I had believed
That I would see the goodness of the Lord
In the land of the living.
14 Wait on the Lord;
Be of good courage,
And He shall strengthen your heart;
Wait, I say, on the Lord!

When my situation and life looked HOPELESS, I held on to this beautiful promise from the Lord. I chose to BELIEVE that I would see the goodness of the Lord in the land of the living.

My life was NOT over, despite what it looked and felt like at the time. And I can tell you, that over the past seven years, I have seen, in countless ways, the goodness of the Lord revealed to me. He is faithful, He is merciful, and He is good!

Daniel 11:35 (NIV)

35 Some of the wise will stumble, so that they may be refined, purified and made spotless until the time of the end, for it will still come at the appointed time.

I had stumbled and fallen, but God promised to refine, purify and make me spotless until the time of the end, for it (God's plan for my life) will still come and be fulfilled.

Galatians 6:1-2 Amplified Bible, Classic Edition (AMPC)

Brethren, if any person is overtaken in misconduct or sin of any sort, you who are spiritual [who are responsive to and controlled by the Spirit] should set him right and restore and reinstate him, without any sense of superiority and with all gentleness, keeping an attentive eye on yourself, lest you should be tempted also.

The Lord spoke to me from this passage in Galatians that my restoration would be a process, and would take time. The first thing was to be "set right". When a bone is broken, before it can begin to heal, and so that it will heal properly, it has to be SET. I broke my arm when I was about 11 years old. I remember how painful it was for the doctor to "set the bone". For me the "setting right" was about confession and repentance, not only privately before God, but to my family, and publicly, to my church and all those I had failed. That was a painful process, but necessary, so that I could heal correctly.

The next part of the process was to RESTORE. I needed time to heal, to assess where I was at, and how I had gotten there, and make the adjustments necessary to keep me from failing again.

Thankfully I had a few spiritual leaders, and especially my Pastor, Larry Moss who stood with me, prayed for me and helped guide me through this process.

69

The final step was REINSTATEMENT. I had stepped down from ministry for a time, to focus on the "setting right" and "restoring" parts of the process. Finally, it was time to be REINSTATED.

Thankfully, my church family received me with open arms. There are many more that I could list, but I will conclude with this one…

Micah 7:8-9, 18-19 NKJV

8 Do not rejoice over me, my enemy;

When I fall, I will arise;

When I sit in darkness,

The LORD will be a light to me.

9 I will bear the indignation of the LORD,

Because I have sinned against Him,

Until He pleads my case

And executes justice for me.

He will bring me forth to the light;

I will see His righteousness.

18 Who is a God like You,

Pardoning iniquity

And passing over the transgression of the remnant of His heritage?

He does not retain His anger forever,

Because He delights in mercy.

19 He will again have compassion on us,

And will subdue our iniquities.
You will cast all our sins into the depths of the sea.

This, along with the experience I related in Chapter 7, from Zechariah 3, gave me such encouragement, that God was on my side, silencing the shaming accusations of Satan against me.

The Bible says in 1 John that we have an advocate with the Father, Jesus Christ the righteous!

An advocate is a defense attorney! Jesus is our defense attorney in the Court of Heaven, and He has never lost a case!

I pray that these scriptures, and the message of this book will encourage you to not give up, butto trust that God can bring restoration and healing into your life, for your good and His glory!

Printed in the USA
CPSIA information can be obtained
at www.ICGtesting.com
LVHW011235111023
760703LV00011B/838